FOOD ENGINEERING

FROM CONCEPT TO CONSUMER

BY MICHAEL BURGAN

CHILDREN'S PRESS®

An Imprint of Scholastic Inc.

CONTENT CONSULTANT
Matthew Cael, Certified Food Scientist

PHOTOGRAPHS ©: cover: Wolfgang Flamisch/Media Bakery; 2-3: Erik Isakson/Media Bakery; 4 left: Mediablitzimages/Alamy Images; 4 right: Clare Gaine/Alamy Images; 5 left: The Star-Ledger/Jerry McCrea/The Image Works; 5 right: wavebreakmedia/Shutterstock, Inc.; 6-7: The Granger Collection; 8: Joshua Resnick/Shutterstock, Inc.; 9: HLPhoto/Shutterstock, Inc.; 10 left: Hulton Archive/Stringer/Getty Images; 10 right: Mediablitzimages/Alamy Images; 11: Erik Isakson/Media Bakery; 12: Everett Historical/Shutterstock, Inc.; 13: TopFoto/ The Image Works; 14 left: The Spencer Family Archives; 14 right: Phanie/Superstock, Inc.; 15: aquariagirl1970/Shutterstock, Inc.; 16: H. Armstrong Roberts/ClassicStock/The Image Works; 17: Michael Neelon (misc)/Alamy Images; 18-19: epa european pressphoto agency b.v./Alamy Images; 20: Clare Gaine/Alamy Images; 21: Roger Davies/Alamy Images; 22 left: AP Images; 22 right-23 left: Interfoto/Alamy Images; 23 right: akg-images/The Image Works; 24: Guenter Beer/VISUM/The Image Works; 25: Robyn Beck/Getty Images; 26: Tim Robbins/Media Bakery; 27: Randy Faris/Media Bakery; 28: The Image Works; 29: Media Bakery/Media Bakery; 30: David Parry/EMPPL PA Wire/AP Images; 31: margouillat photo/Shutterstock, Inc.; 32-33: age fotostock/Superstock, Inc.; 34: Zuma Press, Inc./ Alamy Images; 35: The Star-Ledger/Jerry McCrea/The Image Works; 36: Sergio Ponomarev/ Shutterstock, Inc.; 37: Anastasios71/Shutterstock, Inc.; 40: Bob Daemmrich/The Image Works; 41: Christian Draghici/Shutterstock, Inc.; 42: Greg Tsaknakis (Creative Director)/Kostas Kaparos (Designer & Illustrator)/; 43 top: Eugenio Marongiu/Shutterstock, Inc.; 43 bottom: BirchTree/Alamy Images; 44: David Frazier/The Images Works; 45, 46-47: wavebreakmedia/ Shutterstock, Inc.; 48: Stock Connection/Superstock, Inc.; 49: Monty Rakusen/Media Bakery; 50 left: Marc Bruxelle/Shutterstock, Inc.; 50 right: Tribune Content Agency LLC/Alamy Images; 51 top: Aneta_Gu/Shutterstock, Inc.; 51 bottom: Steve Karnowski/AP Images; 52: science photo/Shutterstock, Inc.; 53: Evru/Shutterstock, Inc.; 54: Steve Skjold/Alamy Images; 55: Science Source; 56: Sakarin Sawasdinaka/Shutterstock, Inc.; 56: Sakarin Sawasdinaka/ Shutterstock, Inc.; 57: Rob Byron/Shutterstock, Inc.; 58 left: phototy/Shutterstock, Inc.; 58 right: View Stock/Alamy Images; 59: Viktor Fischer/Alamy Images.

LIBRARY OF CONGRESS CATALOGING-IN-PUBLICATION DATA
Burgan, Michael, author.
  Food engineering : from concept to consumer / by Michael Burgan.
      pages cm. — (Calling all innovators : a career for you)
  Summary: "Learn about the history of food engineering and find out what it takes to make it in this exciting career field." — Provided by publisher.
  Includes bibliographical references and index.
  ISBN 978-0-531-21898-3 (library binding) — ISBN 978-0-531-21916-4 (pbk.)
1. Food industry and trade — Juvenile literature. 2. Food industry and trade — Vocational guidance — Juvenile literature. 3. Food engineers — Juvenile literature. 4. Food — Biotechnology — Juvenile literature. I. Title. II. Series: Calling all innovators.
  TP370.3.B87 2015
  664 — dc23   2015002480

All rights reserved. Published in 2016 by Children's Press, an imprint of Scholastic Inc.
Printed in the United States of America 113

1 2 3 4 5 6 7 8 9 10 R 25 24 23 22 21 20 19 18 17 16

CALLING ALL INNOVATORS

A CAREER FOR YOU

Science, technology, engineering, arts, and math are the fields that drive innovation. Whether they are finding ways to make our lives easier or developing the latest entertainment, the people who work in these fields are changing the world for the better. Do you have what it takes to join the ranks of today's greatest innovators? Read on to discover if a career in the exciting world of food engineering is for you.

TABLE *of* CONTENTS

Flash freezing techniques have made it easier to distribute out-of-season foods throughout the world.

The hybrid TomTato plant can grow tomatoes and potatoes at the same time.

Flavor chemists combine chemicals to give foods new and interesting tastes.

Food science plays a major role in fresh and processed foods alike.

A 1966 ad for Tang focuses on the drink's use by astronauts.

The Gemini Astronauts drank Tang...like this.
You can drink it from a glass.

The Gemini Astronauts drank Tang in space. Tang has been carried on the Gemini flights . . . including the 7/6 rendezvous mission. Tang is the instant breakfast drink with more vitamin C and A – more than orange juice, tomato juice or any juice. And Tang with natural orange flavor is the breakfast drink your whole family will go for. Mix them some Tang tomorrow morning.

Demonstration photograph. Gemini simulator, courtesy McDonnell Aircraft.

GF
GENERAL FOODS
KITCHENS

CHAPTER ONE

CREATING THE FOOD WE EAT

The earliest astronauts encountered many challenges as they traveled through space. Among the obstacles they faced was figuring out an effective way to eat and drink aboard their spacecraft. Space lacks gravity. As a result, things float around in a spaceship. A spilled drop of a drink could easily sail into the spacecraft's sensitive electronic equipment. This could damage the system, possibly endangering the astronauts' lives.

In 1962, astronaut John Glenn tested out a drink made by mixing water with an orange powder called Tang. Glenn sucked the sugary, fruit-flavored drink out of a plastic tube so it wouldn't spill. Like the other equipment that made space travel possible, this powder was the product of scientific research and engineering. It was created in 1957 in the lab of a food scientist named William Mitchell. Working for a major food company, Mitchell also helped invent such products as Jell-O and Cool Whip.

FOOD SCIENCE FIRSTS

1804	1924	1946	1980
Tin cans are first used to store meat.	Clarence Birdseye creates the modern method of freezing foods.	Popcorn is first cooked using a microwave.	Juice is first sold in single-serving boxes with straws.

A LONG HISTORY

Thousands of years before Mitchell created Tang, early humans experimented with food. These people were not scientists. However, they sometimes accidentally discovered new ways to prepare and **preserve** food. Their discoveries rested on facts of nature that today's food scientists still use.

The earliest form of food science is the simple act of cooking. Grilling a freshly killed animal made the meat easier to chew and **digest**. People later learned that drying meat slowly could keep it from rotting. Adding salt to foods was another way to preserve them.

Early cooks in Central America mixed corn kernels with the chemical called lime when making a corn flour called masa. They discovered that the lime made the kernels easier to grind. What they didn't know was that it also released helpful **nutrients** in the corn.

For thousands of years, people have cooked meat by grilling it over open flames.

AIR BUBBLES FORM AS YEAST RELEASES GAS DURING RISING PROCESS

Yeast is an integral ingredient in most kinds of bread.

MORE ANCIENT METHODS

For more than 7,000 years, people have used yeast to create new foods or improve their cooking. Yeast is made up of **microorganisms** that float through the air. Adding yeast to grains and water causes bread to rise. The rising process creates a lighter, fluffier bread than the flatbreads humans first ate. Humans discovered this by mistake several thousand years ago, when yeast fell into a flatbread mixture before it was baked. The first wine was probably an accident, too. Yeast might have come in contact with grape juice. It then fed on sugar in the juice, turning the sugar into alcohol. This process is called **fermentation**. Other microorganisms, such as **bacteria**, can also ferment foods, helping preserve them.

Bacteria can also start chemical reactions that create whole new foods. Cheese was first made when people used the stomachs of cows and other animals to carry milk. Bacteria in the milk combined with chemicals naturally found in the stomachs. This caused the milk to separate into solids called curds and a liquid called whey. The solid curds were the source of the cheese.

PAST MARVELS

Clarence Birdseye's innovations made it possible for people to eat their favorite foods year-round.

CLARENCE BIRDSEYE AND HIS QUICK FREEZE MACHINE

A young biologist named Clarence Birdseye headed to Labrador, Canada, in 1912 to trade animal furs. While he was there, he made a discovery that changed the history of **processed** foods.

Birdseye witnessed native Inuit people freezing their freshly caught fish on ice in extremely cold weather. When they later defrosted and ate the fish, it looked and tasted almost exactly as if it were fresh.

THE SCIENCE OF "FLASH FREEZING"

Freezing food slowly or at higher temperatures causes it to lose flavor and turn mushy. While watching the Inuits work, Birdseye realized that fresh food would not be ruined if it was frozen very quickly at extreme temperatures. While still in Canada, he experimented by freezing cabbage so his family could eat it all year long.

Today, there are a huge number of frozen foods to choose among.

Almost all grocery stores have freezer cases today.

After returning to the United States, Birdseye began experimenting with different ways to "flash freeze" fish and other foods. In 1924, he perfected his Quick Freeze Machine. He used it to freeze fish, fruit, and vegetables and then sold them at grocery stores. At first, consumers were not eager to try Birdseye's food. They assumed it would taste just as bad as earlier forms of frozen food. But as people tried Birdseye's food, they learned what he had discovered in icy Labrador: flash freezing preserved the food's taste and texture almost perfectly.

SPREADING THE WORD

To convince more stores to sell his food, Birdseye invented a special display case that would keep frozen food from melting. Refrigerated railroad cars carried the food to stores across the country. As time passed, other food companies began flash freezing a wider variety of food.

Using his training as a scientist, Birdseye made it possible for almost any food to be frozen and shipped thousands of miles without losing its flavor. In addition, seasonal fruits and vegetables could easily be enjoyed year-round. Thanks to Birdseye's innovations, frozen foods remain a common sight in supermarkets around the world. ✺

Louis Pasteur's methods made dairy products much safer to consume.

KEEPING FOOD FRESH

Modern food science began developing a few hundred years ago. It drew on research from several branches of science, including chemistry, biology, and physics. A major concern of the time was finding ways to keep food fresh. In the early 19th century, French ruler Napoleon Bonaparte needed to feed his soldiers when they were far from their camps. French chef Nicolas Appert found that canning and briefly heating foods preserved them. A tightly sealed can prevented bacteria from **contaminating** the food inside.

Later in the century, scientist Louis Pasteur discovered another way to keep foods safe and fresh. His process, called pasteurization, involved heating and then chilling liquids such as milk. This method is still used today to kill harmful organisms in dairy products. The foods are heated at temperatures between 145 and 302 degrees Fahrenheit (63 and 150 degrees Celsius) for as little as 4 seconds or as long as 20 minutes.

PACKING UP

In the United States, food companies of the late 19th century wanted to ship their products across the country. This led them to develop new ways of producing and packaging food. One example came in the meatpacking industry. The Cudahy Packing Company combined old food science with new technology. The company's specialty was curing, or preserving, pork using salt or sugar. The company started doing this in refrigerated rooms, which allowed it to produce bacon year-round. Without refrigeration, the meat would have spoiled during the curing process.

Brothers John Harvey Kellogg and Will Keith Kellogg invented corn flakes in 1898. Later they learned that the natural oil in corn made the flakes spoil quickly. Most of this oil was found in a part of the corn called the germ. Removing the germ left a corn product that lasted longer and tasted better. Cereal makers also began adding sugar and malt to help the cereal stay crisp in milk.

Cereal has been a popular breakfast food for more than a century.

FIRST THINGS FIRST

Percy Spencer's microwave oven made heating food faster and easier than ever.

A NEW WAY TO COOK

Today, many people rely on the microwave oven to quickly heat everything from popcorn to leftovers. This remarkably useful device was invented by scientist Percy Spencer. In 1946, Spencer was working with microwaves, a form of energy. During World War II (1939–1945), the U.S. and British governments had used microwaves as part of radar systems. These systems relied on a device called a cavity magnetron, which was fairly small and could produce large amounts of microwaves.

Spencer worked for a company that made magnetrons. One day in the lab, he stood near one of these devices as it was producing microwaves. Soon after, he noticed that some chocolate in his pocket had melted. Spencer realized that the energy from the magnetron had melted it. From this, he determined that microwaves could be used to heat food.

HOW IT WORKS

All food has at least some water inside of it. Microwave ovens work by heating this water. Even a kernel of popcorn has enough water in it to be heated by the waves and then pop. The more water a food has in it, the faster it will heat up in a microwave.

Today, it is rare to find a kitchen without a microwave oven.

Microwaves pass through glass, plastic, or paper containers to heat the food inside. However, most metals can't be put into microwave ovens. This is because microwave energy bounces off them and can set the food on fire or damage the oven. Some special metal foils, however, absorb the energy and help the food cook. They are added to the food's packaging.

MICROWAVES IN THE KITCHEN

The first microwave ovens were huge and used only in restaurants. By the 1970s, they had shrunk enough in size to become popular in homes. In response, food companies began developing foods that were meant to be cooked in microwave ovens. Food scientists had to consider such things as how much water was in these products. Adding salt or other ingredients can also influence the cooking time. Today's food scientists still work to make sure that packaged microwaveable foods heat quickly and evenly and taste good. ☀

Food manufacturers must carefully balance the ingredients in microwaveable meals.

THE GROWING ROLE OF FOOD SCIENCE

Producing and selling packaged food became a huge business in the United States during the 20th century. In the 1920s, flour maker General Mills opened a test kitchen to create new recipes using its products. It then shared the best recipes with the public. This encouraged people to use General Mills products, helping the company grow to become one of the world's largest food manufacturers.

Meanwhile, scientists sought new ingredients and ways to process food. The goal was to make tastier products than their competitors. For example, a sweet syrup made from corn gave some baked goods a better texture. The syrup was a **carbohydrate**, one of the three basic kinds of food nutrients. The other two are **protein** and fat. Some foods contain all three, and food scientists mix them in different ways to create different tastes and shape a food's nutritional value.

Canned soup, breakfast cereal, and other convenient new foods changed the way people ate during the mid-20th century.

Food companies began offering processed foods with fewer calories in the 1980s.

CHANGING DIETS

After the end of World War II in 1945, Americans had more money on average than they'd had in almost two decades. They were eager to spend it on new food products, especially ones that were easy to prepare. For example, boxed mixes for cakes and cookies only required cooks to add some water and perhaps an egg. Frozen meals required cooks to do little other than heat them in the oven or microwave.

The rise of convenient packaged foods increased the amount people ate. It also led people to eat more unhealthy ingredients. For example, fats and oils are commonly added to processed foods to improve flavor. However, they can increase the risk of heart disease and other illnesses. During the 1970s, the average American ate 53 pounds (24 kilograms) per year of fats and oils that were added to foods. By the 1990s, this had increased to 66 pounds (30 kg).

By the 1980s, many people were expressing concern about the amount of fat in processed foods. Food scientists responded by creating new products that had less fat but still tasted good. For example, 1981 saw the introduction of Lean Cuisine. These frozen meals had smaller portions and less fat than other frozen dishes. Some companies created fat substitutes. These substances gave food some of the texture and taste of real fats, but had fewer **calories**.

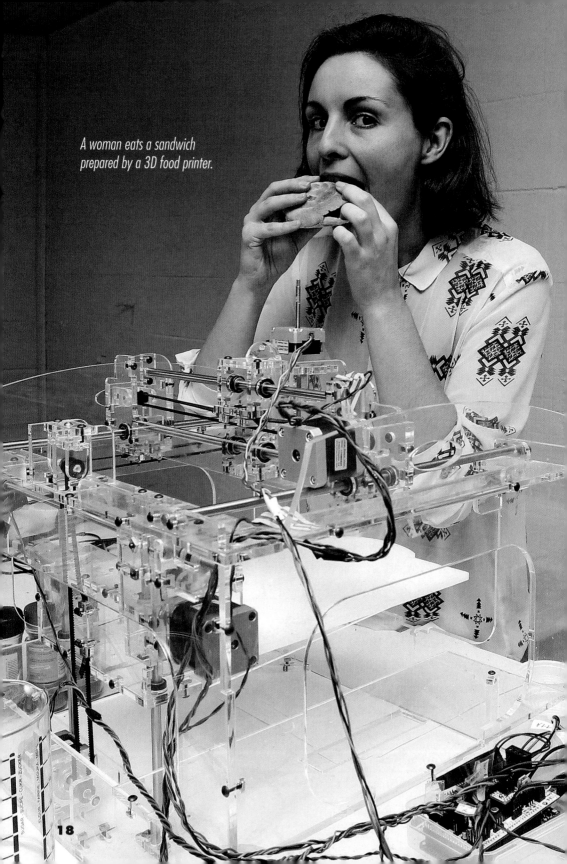

A woman eats a sandwich prepared by a 3D food printer.

CHAPTER TWO

TODAY AND TOMORROW

I n 2006, Kentucky high school student Noy Schaal discovered that she could create tasty shapes and images using chocolate—and a 3D printer. The same computer technology used to make everything from machine parts to artificial limbs can also make food.

Making food with a computer is more than just a fun hobby. The National Aeronautics and Space Administration (NASA) plans to use 3D food printers in space. Such machines could also enable cooks to easily alter recipes to suit different eaters. For example, they could remove fat from a meal for someone who is on a diet.

Computers that can create tasty meals are just one of the many recent developments in food science technology. Today's food scientists are always working to create interesting new products and ways to process food.

CREATING NEW CROPS

Early 1900s	1905	1950s	1994
Scientist Luther Burbank creates the plumcot, a cross between a plum and an apricot.	George Harrison Shull experiments with hybrid corn, which increases the amount of corn that can be grown in an area of land.	Norman Borlaug crossbreeds different kinds of wheat to create a new type that resists disease and grows in a wide range of environments.	Scientists create the first GMO crop, a tomato that stays fresh longer than regular tomatoes.

TomTato plants grow tomatoes above the soil and potatoes belowground.

HIGH AND LOW TECH IN THE LABS

While food scientists explore new technology such as 3D printers, they also sometimes use old methods to create new foods or crops. Two examples come from agriculture.

Farmers have long used a process called grafting to create new crops. Grafting is when a branch from one plant or tree is attached to another growing plant. The new branch goes where an old one was cut from the original plant. Both the branch and the plant have a layer of cells called cambium. These cells help a cut tree heal. They also help the grafted branch become part of the host plant. The plant then has its own traits along with those of the grafted branch.

Farmers can use grafting to grow a single plant that produces two or more kinds of fruit. One modern product of grafting is the TomTato. Introduced in 2013, it combines a tomato plant with a potato plant and is able to produce both crops. The TomTato could appeal to people who want to raise their own food but have limited space.

MIXING IT UP

Crossbreeding is another old agricultural technique that is still used today. Seeds from a plant with one trait are mixed with pollen from a related plant with a different trait. The plant that grows from these seeds has both traits. For example, a crossbreed between a plant with sweet fruit and a plant with large fruit might produce fruit that is both sweet and large.

There are many examples of crossbred crops in grocery stores today. Plant breeders combined wheat and rye to create a grain called triticale. The pluot is a crossbreed of a plum and an apricot. In 2013, California plant scientists crossbred two kinds of grapes. The result was a green grape that tastes like cotton candy!

Crossbreeding is also used to produce meat. Cattle have been crossbred with American buffalo to create an animal called a beefalo. Beefalo are cheaper to raise than cattle are. They can also live in a wider range of temperatures and do not get sick as often as cattle do.

Though they look like regular green grapes, this variety has the flavor of cotton candy.

FROM THIS TO THAT

Ancel Keys's food research led to the creation of the K ration.

FOOD ON THE GO

Meeting the dining needs of soldiers has often fueled changes in food production and storage. During World War II, the U.S. military sent millions of people overseas to fight. The troops needed nutritious food to complete their difficult jobs. They also needed meals that would not spoil quickly and could be eaten easily when they were far from kitchens.

THE K RATION

Based on the research of a scientist named Ancel Keys, the U.S. Army created a package of food called the K ration. The new product was made up of three separate meals that contained such foods as chocolate, canned meats and cheese, and chewing gum. One K ration provided all of the nutrients a soldier needed each day.

K rations also came with instant coffee, a powder that soldiers mixed with water. Instant coffees had been around for years. In one process invented just before the war, brewed coffee was sprayed into heated towers. The heat turned the sprayed liquid into a powder.

IMPROVING MILITARY MEALS

By the 1980s, the U.S. military wanted portable food for soldiers that was lighter to carry and stayed fresher longer. Borrowing ideas from the foods used to feed astronauts, scientists created new types of rations called meals ready to eat (MREs). These portable meals gave soldiers a greater variety of food choices. Scientists have continued to improve the product ever since its introduction. Modern MREs even come with their own "oven." Water is combined with special chemicals in a pouch to create heat that warms the meal. ✹

Early rations were packaged in a variety of tins, bottles, and wrappers.

Soldiers eat their rations aboard a ship prior to the invasion of Normandy during World War II.

SOME TYPICAL MRES

Chicken with noodles
Nut raisin mix with chocolate
Peanut butter
Jelly or jam
Wheat snack bread
Beverage
Hot sauce

Beef ravioli
Cheese spread
Wheat snack bread
Corn nuts
Dried fruit
Beverage
Hot sauce

Vegetable lasagna
Wet pack fruit
Cookie
Peanut butter
Crackers
Candy
Beverage
Seasoning

NEW FOODS FROM THE LAB

Crossbreeding is based on the science of genetics. Genes are chemicals in all living things that shape their appearance and other traits. Parents' genes mix together to determine what their offspring will look like.

In food science, genetic engineering usually involves taking genes from one **species** and putting them into another. The new genes give the target species a new trait. At times, scientists might also alter genes already found in the animal or plant.

The results of this process are called genetically modified organisms (GMOs). The first GMO food, the Flavr Savr tomato, appeared in grocery stores in 1994. Scientists altered one of the genes in a tomato species so its fruit would not become soft after it was picked and shipped to stores.

Today, most of the corn and soybeans grown in the United States are GMOs. Genetic modifications help protect these crops from the negative effects of **pesticides**. Other crops are modified to help them resist diseases or produce more nutrients.

A scientist cares for a genetically modified tomato plant.

Labels allow consumers to choose whether or not they want to purchase GMO products.

PROS AND CONS

One example of a crop that was modified to be more nutritious is golden rice. The rice is named for its deep yellow color, which comes from the nutrient beta-carotene. The human body uses this nutrient to produce vitamin A. A gene from a carrot plant was added to the rice to give it beta-carotene. Golden rice could save lives in parts of the world where people lack vitamin A in their diets.

GMO crops offer other benefits, too. Farmers can grow more crops than before while using less water and fewer pesticides. Some scientists believe that GMOs might be the only way to produce enough food to feed Earth's growing population.

However, some people don't like the idea of genetically modified foods. They think the altered crops could harm their health or affect the natural growth of non-GMO plants. Many people want food companies to label products containing GMOs. Some nations have even outlawed the growing of GMO crops altogether.

The best way to get most types of nutrients is to eat fresh foods that have not been processed.

NATURAL NUTRIENTS

Another branch of food science aims to process foods in ways that allow more of a plant's helpful natural chemicals to stay in the product. These chemicals are known as phytonutrients. *Phyto* is the Greek word for "plant." Phytonutrients can lower a person's risk of developing heart disease and other illnesses.

Several types of phytonutrients are found in common foods. Carrots, spinach, and tomatoes contain carotenoids. These phytonutrients improve eye health and reduce a person's risk of developing certain cancers. Citrus fruits, apples, and green tea contain phytonutrients called flavonoids. These chemicals reduce a person's risk of asthma and arthritis.

In 2014, a Swiss chocolate company introduced new products that were high in a helpful phytonutrient found in cocoa beans— the raw ingredient in cocoa powder and chocolate. The chemical improves the flow of blood in the body. After seven years of experiments, scientists at the company had found a way to get more of the phytonutrient into chocolate products.

ADDED ADVANTAGES

Today's food scientists also look to make healthier products by adding nutrients to existing products. For example, some companies use a food **additive** that lowers cholesterol, a chemical linked to heart disease. This helpful substance is made from plants and can be used in a wide range of foods, from pudding to salad dressings.

One frequently studied fruit is the blueberry. Its phytonutrients can lower blood pressure and perhaps lower a person's risk of developing cancer. Food companies are putting blueberries, or powder and juice made from them, into more products.

Antioxidants are another common additive to processed foods. These substances attack chemicals in the body called free radicals, which can damage healthy cells.

Blueberries contain a number of nutrients that can improve a person's health.

MODERN MARVEL

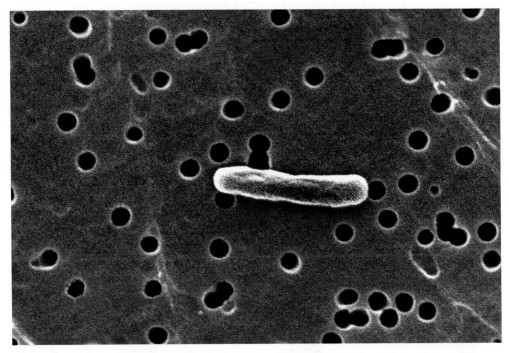

Though E.coli bacteria are incredibly small, they can cause huge health problems when consumed.

MAKING FOODS SAFER

Keeping food fresh and safe to eat is a major concern of food companies. One problem is that harmful bacteria can develop in food as it is transported from factories to stores. This can result in customers purchasing food that has already gone bad. To help avoid this issue, scientists are working on new ways to detect these bacteria more easily.

CHANGING COLOR TO SHOW DANGER

"Smart labels" are made using a material that changes appearance when it comes into contact with certain harmful bacteria, such as *E. coli* and salmonella. People who eat foods containing these bacteria can become very ill or even die. The labels are placed inside individual packages of meat. Depending on the label, it might change color or turn from clear to cloudy when it detects bacteria. The labels can also detect changes in temperature that might indicate a food has spoiled. They can even detect if the packaging has broken in some way, which could also lead to spoilage. Such labels would allow grocery stores to dispose of spoiled food before it is sold. They would also provide customers with an easy way to see if the food has gone bad while sitting in the refrigerator.

DETECTING OTHER THREATS

Another danger in foods is the presence of listeria. This bacteria can contaminate many different kinds of foods and cause serious illness. In 2014, researchers in Australia revealed a new way to detect listeria in food before it is packaged. It relies on a process called mass spectrometry, which uses lasers to detect the presence of certain chemicals. This new process will make it much faster for food companies to scan their products for the presence of listeria. It is also able to detect very low levels of the bacteria compared to older testing methods. ☀

New food labels would enable customers to be sure that their meat is safe to eat.

NEW SOURCES OF NUTRITION

What do you think meat made by humans in a laboratory would taste like? In 2013, three people found out when they tested the first hamburger cooked with meat grown from cow cells. The burger was drier than a regular one because the lab-grown meat lacked the fat found in natural meat. However, the tasters agreed that it was a good start for the new product. The food scientist who grew the meat is still working to improve it and make it cheaper to produce. But within a few years, people might be able to buy lab-grown meat in stores. Producing beef this way might mean that fewer cows will be killed and less space will be needed to raise livestock.

A product called Soylent is another new food from the lab. Its creator aimed to make a food that was easy to prepare and provided all the nutrition a person needs. Soylent comes as a powder that is mixed with water. It contains carbohydrates, protein, and fats, as well as vitamins and minerals, and is made entirely from plant products. Each serving of Soylent is meant to replace an entire meal.

As part of a demonstration, a chef prepares a hamburger made from lab-grown meat.

LAB-GROWN MEAT LOOKS JUST LIKE A HAMBURGER MADE FROM NATURAL MEAT

THIN EDIBLE SKIN
HOLDS LIQUID INSIDE

Chefs can use chemical processes to put almost any flavors inside round, edible containers.

PERFECTING PACKAGING

Someday you might be able to drink a bottle of water and then eat
the container it came in. Scientists are currently developing ways
of creating edible bottles. Certain chemicals can turn liquids into
spheres that pop when they are chewed. This method is sometimes
used by creative chefs to form unique dishes. It might also be useful
in creating edible containers. Another possible process uses plantlike
life-forms called algae to create a "skin" around a serving of water.
The final product looks a little like a jellyfish.

Another new kind of food packaging comes from sugarcane. It
is formed using a plastic made from ethanol, a fuel that comes from
sugarcane and other plants. Manufacturing this type of packaging
causes less harm to the environment than traditional plastics, which
are made from oil. Like other plastics, the sugarcane packaging can
be recycled.

Creating new foods is all about experimentation. Here, food scientists test the effect of liquid nitrogen on citrus fruit.

CHAPTER THREE

MAKING GOOD FOOD

When people eat cupcakes, they usually start by peeling away the paper liner and throwing it away. But in 2009, a group of Purdue University students thought of a way to end that task and save paper. They created cupcake liners made from soybeans. After the cupcakes are baked, you can eat the liner along with the treat.

The students took part in one of several contests held each year to give future food scientists a chance to experiment. The team included students studying food process engineering, food manufacturing, and **biochemistry**. Their edible cupcake liners never made it into stores. But other student contest winners have caught the eye of food companies.

PRIZEWINNING STUDENT FOOD PROJECTS

1995	1998	2007	2013
Pizza Pop Ups — mini pizzas that can be cooked in a toaster	Wrapidos — tortillas with fillings that don't leak when they are cooked	Chicken Noodle Bites — broth and soup ingredients together inside a dough pocket	Squashetti — pasta made from squash

Students who want to become food scientists should study subjects such as chemistry in college.

CAREERS IN FOOD SCIENCE AND TECHNOLOGY

Student contests show that many different kinds of scientists and engineers work together to create new ingredients, flavors, foods, and packaging. While they all fall under the general label of food scientists, these innovators have a wide range of skills and specialties.

Whether they specialize in designing new foods, improving old ones, or ensuring food safety, food scientists and engineers usually study for many years before they begin working. Most start by attending a four-year college or university to earn a bachelor's degree. In food science courses, they learn how the principles of chemistry, biology, and other fields relate to the food industry.

After completing a bachelor's degree, many future food scientists continue their education. Advanced degrees are required for many positions in the food science industry. They are also required for people who want to work at colleges and teach others about food science.

COMMON FOOD ADDITIVES

Name	Use
Acetic acid	Preservative
Casein	Thickener
Cellulose gum	Thickener and stabilizer
Sodium benzoate	Preservative
Glycerin	Sweetener
Pectin	Thickener

FOOD CHEMISTS

Chemistry is the foundation of any food scientist's education. Some students pursue this field even further and become specialized food chemists. Every food has a range of chemicals in it that shape its taste, texture, and smell. Table sugar, for example, is the chemical sucrose. Food chemists know how much sugar can dissolve in a certain amount of liquid and at what temperature it melts. That knowledge shapes how much sugar might be added to some packaged foods.

Chemicals can be solids, liquids, or gases. Food chemists usually work with the first two. They study how solids and liquids interact. For example, a liquid ingredient may be combined with a solid to make a dessert that can be packaged and stored in the refrigerator. Or a chemical such as citric acid might be added to a food to preserve it. Other chemical additives might enhance a food's flavor or give it a certain color. Some additives occur naturally, while others are created in labs.

A flavor chemist works to create a caramel flavor for coffee.

FOOD MICROBIOLOGIST

A biologist studies the many different forms of life on Earth. A food microbiologist specializes in microorganisms, such as bacteria and viruses, and how they relate to food. The harmful creatures that can make people sick are called **pathogens**. Other microorganisms can cause food to decline in quality over time. Some microorganisms can also be helpful, such as bacteria called probiotics.

Microbiologists work for food makers or do research at universities. Some also work for government departments that ensure food safety. Their goal is to study how microorganisms grow and survive in food and how to keep harmful ones out. Part of the scientists' work is to help create foods that can safely remain on shelves for long periods of time. They also look for better ways to store and package food to reduce the risk of pathogens developing.

Microbiologists use microscopes to examine tiny life-forms that cannot be seen with the naked eye.

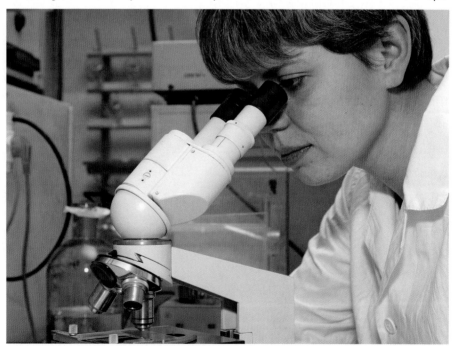

Yogurt contains many microorganisms that offer health benefits when consumed.

FERMENTATION SCIENTIST

Like microbiologists, fermentation scientists study microorganisms. However, they focus entirely on the helpful life-forms that create fermented foods. An estimated one-third of all the foods humans eat are fermented. Pickles, yogurt, and some types of bread and cheese are all examples of foods that rely on fermentation.

The basic process of fermentation involves using microorganisms to convert the sugar in foods into other substances. Fermentation scientists learn about how these microorganisms live, the conditions that affect their behavior, and how fermentation affects a food's taste. This allows them to determine exactly which kinds of microorganisms are best suited to different tasks. For example, they know that the kind of yeast that creates great bread might not work well for turning grape juice into wine. When making dairy products such as cheese or sour cream, the bacteria used can affect the food's taste and smell. Certain bacteria might also destroy other microorganisms that can spoil the finished product.

AN INTERVIEW WITH FOOD SCIENTIST MATTHEW CAEL

Matthew Cael is a Certified Food Scientist who began working in the field in 2012. Here are some of his thoughts on his career.

When did you become interested in being a food scientist? During my junior year of high school. At the time, I was taking a culinary class, and we watched a video on food industry professions where there was a brief discussion of food science. I have always had a love of science and a passion for food, so it was the perfect combination for me!

What kind of classes did you take before, during, and after high school and college to prepare for your career? In high school, I took a lot of science and math courses, with a mix of some specialty culinary courses that were offered at my high school, just for fun. In college, we had two different tracks that one could take depending on where he or she wanted to go in the industry. These two tracks were the "science option" or the "industry option." The science option was heavy in advanced science and math courses, and was designed for people who intended to go to graduate school.

The industry option focused more on showing you different skills and techniques across the food industry, such as meat science, dairy science, and fruits and vegetable processing.

After my undergraduate degree, I went to graduate school, where I specialized in ingredient technology for food processing.

What other projects and jobs did you do in school to prepare you for what you do now? When I went to college, I worked in the dining halls as a manager, where I led a team of 25 students to run 12 different themed food lines per night. This experience gave me an understanding of the end use of processed food and the opportunity to learn about food preparation and safety.

I moved from the kitchen to a research position in the Department of Animal and Food Science, where I helped graduate students and professors with their research projects. This was a great influence on my decision to attend graduate school and perform research. I interned for the On The Border and Chili's brands in culinary research and development when I was a junior in college. I worked with a team of chefs and food scientists to create new dishes in a test kitchen, transition them to a food manufacturer to make larger quantities, and then figure out how to present them consistently in 2,500 restaurants every day. This job gave me the chance to understand how to work with a diverse team of chefs, scientists, businesspeople, and manufacturers, which transitioned perfectly into my current job.

What are some of the specific academic paths that can lead to a job in your field? I studied food science for my chosen academic path during college and graduate school. Many people study chemistry, nutrition, biology, or engineering to get a job in the research side of the food industry. The food industry is global and ever changing, so it takes people from a variety of different backgrounds to make it work.

Do you have a particular project that you're especially proud of or that really took your work to another level? When I was in graduate school, I worked with the Louisiana Sea Grant program and the National Oceanic and Atmospheric Administration on a project using Asian carp, which is an invasive fish species in the United States, to create a canned fish product for earthquake victims in Haiti. This was a unique opportunity to use my scientific skills to contribute to the greater good of other people.

What would your dream job be if you were given unlimited resources? I would open a pizza shop.

What advice would you give a young person who wants to pursue a career in your field? Go for it! Food science is a very unique field, with many different career opportunities. Regardless of what you do in the food industry, it is very rewarding to see a product you have had a hand in making on the store shelf. ✳

A group of food scientists performs a taste test of their company's salsa products.

SENSORY SCIENTIST

Food appeals to all of our senses. Sensory scientists help make foods with as much sensory appeal as possible. At times, they do tests to see how people rate the taste and smell of new foods.

Sensory scientists also research how and why people perceive tastes the way they do. Most people have a taste for sweet and fatty foods, while they generally avoid sour and bitter ones. Yet small amounts of a bitter ingredient can be tasty in certain foods. Sensory scientists help create the proper balance of different tastes in a food. They also explore textures to make foods more appealing. For example, they might test different types of smooth and crunchy peanut butters to find the types that people like best.

CONSUMER BEHAVIOR RESEARCH

How people react to foods sometimes goes beyond simple sensory appeal. Someone's mood can shape her reaction to a new food. So might physical changes in her body that she doesn't even notice. Food scientists who perform consumer behavior research look at a wide range of factors that shape what people choose to eat. For example, they might study how eating foods versus drinking them affects someone's appetite. Or a food company might want to know if adding a certain ingredient will make people feel full more quickly. These scientists' goals include helping food companies make products that are nutritious and that consumers enjoy.

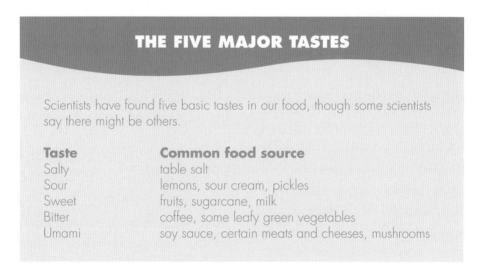

THE FIVE MAJOR TASTES

Scientists have found five basic tastes in our food, though some scientists say there might be others.

Taste	Common food source
Salty	table salt
Sour	lemons, sour cream, pickles
Sweet	fruits, sugarcane, milk
Bitter	coffee, some leafy green vegetables
Umami	soy sauce, certain meats and cheeses, mushrooms

Snack foods such as potato chips are often designed so they do not make people feel full. This encourages people to eat more.

A clean, simple packaging design might help convince consumers that a product is healthy.

CATCHING CONSUMERS' EYES

Packaging food is not just about keeping it safe and making it easy to use. Successful food packaging is also meant to catch consumers' attention and make them want to buy the food. Food companies rely on the work of talented artists to design such packaging. They create designs that are right for a particular food and pleasing to the eye. For example, the Greek design company Mousegraphics worked for food manufacturer Gaea to design new packaging for fruit bars. The designers started by researching other fruit bar packaging so they could create something different. They decided to try for a look that made the fruit bars seem healthy and

natural. The finished package had a simple look—a white background showing the main fruit featured in the bar.

FRESH IDEAS

Not all new packaging actually ends up in the stores. Designers sometimes create test packages that they hope food companies will use in the future. As part of a contest, one designer in Macedonia created a new package for corn chips. Based on the shape of the chips themselves, the cardboard package was made out of a series of triangles. In addition to having an interesting look, this type of package was also able to open easily and close tightly again.

Designers pay very careful attention to which colors they choose for logos and packaging designs.

PROTECTING THE ENVIRONMENT

There's a growing interest in finding ways to make food packaging more **sustainable**. This means creating packaging that can be recycled or is made from recycled goods. Many of today's top packaging designers work hard to find ways of making such packaging attractive to consumers. One recent new product is a paper package for **dehydrated** foods. Not only is the package made from recycled goods, but when water is poured into it, it becomes the bowl for the food! *

Designers also work to create the advertisements that food companies use to promote their products.

FOOD ENGINEERING

Some food scientists focus on the engineering aspect of making food. This involves the processing and packaging of food products. Food can be processed in many ways. Processing can involve steps such as heating a food for pasteurization or flash freezing vegetables. Other processing methods include dehydrating foods to create powders or blending chemicals together to create foods that aren't found in nature. Food engineers help design these processes, as well as the machines used to carry them out. They also help design the machines that put food into packaging and prepare it for shipment. In doing this, they often search for ways to make food manufacturing efficient. This means coming up with new ideas to make processes go faster or use fewer resources.

Engineers design the complex machines used to produce food in factories.

Marketers sometimes use charts and graphs to explain which types of foods are likely to sell well to different types of people.

OTHER JOBS IN FOOD SCIENCE

A college degree in food science can open the door to many jobs that don't directly involve experimenting with new foods. For example, a background in food science can lead to managing a plant where food is produced. Plant managers make sure workers follow all safety and health rules set by the government. Related to that job is quality control. Food companies set their own standards for how their products should look and taste. Quality control workers make sure all the food produced at a plant meets those standards.

Some companies make ingredients that other food companies use to create finished products. These companies rely on sales and marketing professionals to attract clients. Having a background in food science can give these workers an advantage when trying to sell their companies' ingredients. They can explain the value of the ingredients to the food scientists who create foods.

No matter what kind of food you like, food scientists likely played a role in getting it to your family's dinner table.

4

THE PATH TO THE PLATE

Before the rise of food science, most Americans raised and cooked almost everything they ate. Today, most people simply buy their food at grocery stores. Much of this food is packaged and processed in some way. Because food production has become an industry based on science and technology, fewer people are needed to raise crops and livestock. The food produced now is also generally safer than it was in the past.

Stocking the shelves of grocery stores and selling food to consumers is a huge business. In 2013, Americans spent more than $620 billion on food at supermarkets. The typical grocery store carries almost 44,000 different items, and many of them were created by food scientists. Each new product you see at the supermarket went through a long process to get there, with many types of food scientists and engineers playing important roles.

WHEN FAMOUS FOODS HIT STORE SHELVES

1853	1930	1952	1975	1998
Potato chips	Twinkies	Frozen fish sticks	Stove Top stuffing	Splenda sugar substitute

A food scientist experiments with the juice of lemons and oranges.

THE FIRST STEPS

The first step of creating a new food is to come up with an idea for a product that consumers will want to buy. This process might begin with advice from marketing experts, who do research to learn what is already popular. For example, if one type of cookie is very successful, a food company might create new versions of it. Other times, it might want to introduce a completely new product. The company pays attention to new flavors and ingredients popular with consumers and comes up with new foods that feature them.

In either case, the brainstorming of product ideas often involves food scientists who are part of the product development team. This team is responsible for turning ideas into a final product. Other team members might include engineers who can find ways to manufacture a food once an idea has been tested and approved.

Rebecca Skolmutch is a food scientist who has helped create new foods. She says, "There's a food scientist behind every package on the shelf in the market." The same is true of many of the packaged ingredients used in restaurants.

BUILDING A RECIPE

As an idea begins to take shape, a sensory scientist might join in the creative process. For example, a company might want to copy the taste of a competitor's product. Working in a laboratory, sensory scientists use a process called reverse engineering to try to break down the ingredients that give the competition its flavor. They also work with tasters who are specially trained to distinguish different flavors. The results of their tests will help the rest of the team figure out how to bring their idea to life.

The next step is for food scientists and research chefs to go into a research laboratory. There, they create what is called a benchtop formula. This is the basic recipe for a new product. The company will use this recipe to prepare a batch of the new food for testing.

Food scientists test recipes at a biscuit factory.

There are many different types of apples to choose among at most grocery stores.

WHAT'S INSIDE MAKES A DIFFERENCE

Bedford wanted an apple that not only tasted good but could grow well in cold climates. He succeeded, and fans say that the apple's juicy flavor seems to explode in their mouth with every bite. There's a scientific reason for that. The apple's cells are larger than the cells of other apples, so they have more juice. Also, the Honeycrisp's cells shatter when bitten, rather than just fall apart. This is what gives the apple its crisp texture. People like the Honeycrisp so much they're willing to pay more for it than other apples.

CREATING A BETTER APPLE

Even in today's world of high-tech food science, the old methods of grafting and crossbreeding continue. One scientist who has had great success with the old methods is David Bedford of the University of Minnesota. He and other fruit crop research scientists spent 30 years crossbreeding different kinds of apples to create a new, tastier variety. The product of their work is the Honeycrisp apple, which first appeared in 1991. Today, it is one of the most popular kinds of apples in the United States.

David Bedford has played a big role in creating popular new apple varieties.

Honeycrisp apples have a distinctive red, yellow, and green appearance.

A LONG PROCESS

Developing a new apple variety takes time. Working by hand, the scientists take pollen from one kind of apple tree and place it on the blossoming flowers of another type. The seeds that result are planted in greenhouses, and the new trees are eventually moved outside. Then the scientists taste the apples to find the crossbreeds that produce the best fruit. They might spend years judging the apples before they're ready to send a new variety to farmers so they can raise them and sell them.

THE LATEST FLAVORS

Another recent success for Bedford was the SweeTango. It combines the crisp feel of the Honeycrisp with the flavor of another Bedford creation, the Zestar! The SweeTango is proving to be as popular as the Honeycrisp. ✳

A farmer slices into a freshly picked SweeTango apple.

PROTOTYPING A PRODUCT

Creating a benchtop formula is part of the food industry's **prototyping** process. The goal of prototyping is to create a standard recipe that can be used for the final product. The recipe must be something a company can easily use to make the food on a large scale. Research chefs are heavily involved in this process, mixing different ingredients and constantly tasting what they create. As they work, they must keep in mind the company's specific plans for the new product, such as limiting salt or fat.

During prototyping, food scientists help track down the needed ingredients, such as natural flavors and quick-frozen vegetables. They work with companies that make food ingredients for industrial use. The food scientists also identify ingredient functionality. This means figuring out if a certain ingredient will work in the recipe as planned. To make sauces, for example, companies often add starch, a type of carbohydrate, to keep the product thick. But not all kinds of starch might work in a frozen food. The food is cooked and frozen at the plant, then the customer reheats it at home. Some starches lose their ability to thicken the sauce after the second heating.

A food scientist might try several different ingredients to see how they each affect the final product.

The machines used to make processed foods are designed down to the smallest detail.

MICHELE PERCHONOK

Food for astronauts has come a long way since Tang. Michele Perchonok is a NASA food scientist who is helping to provide better meals for today's space missions. Before helping design new foods and packaging for space, she studied chemistry and food science. Perchonok and other NASA food scientists will have a difficult task in the years ahead. One of their main goals is creating foods that can last for up to five years on planned space flights to Mars.

DETERMINING THE DETAILS

As a final recipe gets close to completion, packaging scientists might also join the process. For example, a company might want to sell rice in a large plastic bottle with a handle and spout for easy pouring. The scientists research what kind of plastic would work best for this. Not all plastics can be used in food packaging, and some are better for certain types of food. Packaging scientists also have to figure out how strong the bottle needs to be to hold the desired amount of rice. They use computers to predict how heavy a whole carton of the packages would be. This allows them to ensure that the product can be easily shipped and stored without breaking.

Food engineers also get involved at this stage. They oversee the equipment and techniques actually used to make and process the foods. The engineers first assess whether the company can produce the new product with the equipment they already have. They also determine how costly the product might be.

WHERE THE MAGIC HAPPENS

THE INSTITUTE FOR FOOD SAFETY AND HEALTH

When businesspeople and government officials want the latest information on food safety, they often come to Chicago. The city is the home of the Institute for Food Safety and Health (IFSH), part of the Illinois Institute of Technology.

IFSH scientists often work with scientists from the U.S. Food and Drug Administration (FDA). Together they perfect new ways to keep processed and packaged foods safe. They study such things as microorganisms and food allergies, sometimes working with scientists from food companies. The institute also prepares testing methods that can be used to check food that might be contaminated as part of a terrorist attack. Poisoning the food supply could be one way to harm many people at once.

FOCUS ON NUTRITION

Other scientists study the nutritional value of ingredients and finished foods at the institute's Center for Nutrition Research. Among other things, they try to learn how processing affects a food's nutritional

The Illinois Institute of Technology is home to some of the nation's most prominent food science researchers.

An FDA microbiologist tests food samples for the presence of harmful bacteria.

value and which nutrients promote health. In some tests, human subjects eat certain foods and then scientists measure changes in their weight, blood pressure, and more.

The FDA and other government agencies are concerned with food nutrition because of the strong link between our diets and our health. Eating the right foods can reduce the risk of people developing such conditions as heart disease, high blood pressure, and diabetes.

ENSURING FOOD SAFETY

Food companies can become members of the institute and test if their current methods are the best for producing the safest foods. At times, government scientists step in to make sure the methods meet regulations. All of these scientists work together to fill what institute scientist Richard McDonald calls "knowledge gaps." He said the IFSH, the FDA, and food companies all have the same goal: "Doing whatever we can to protect the American public."

Use-by dates help consumers decide when food is likely to spoil.

TESTING TIME

The next step is called the pilot plant trial. The company begins making larger amounts of the food using the benchtop formula. Food scientists check the product's quality. For example, they examine the food to make sure it looks and tastes the way it should. They also make sure foods are cooked at proper temperatures to kill harmful microorganisms and check that the food is packaged correctly to prevent contamination.

Food scientists also determine the sell-by or use-by dates that will be placed on packages. In some cases, they put the food in chambers that can create various temperatures and levels of humidity. The scientists check the food regularly over a period of time to see how well it lasts under the different conditions.

THE FINAL TWEAKS

Once a food has been deemed safe to eat, sensory scientists bring in groups of consumers to test their reactions to the product. Based on what food testers say about the product, the scientists can make slight changes to the recipe. They might make something less sweet or add more salt.

While those changes go on, the packaging scientists are making sure the packages they designed work as they should. Government regulators check to make sure the packaging displays the required nutrition information. They also make sure the food company is not lying about a product's possible health benefits.

The last testing comes as the food is manufactured on a large scale. Does the finished product taste right? Do the cooking directions on the package produce the desired results? If these final tests come out the way scientists hope, and there are no manufacturing problems, the food is ready to make its way to grocery stores everywhere.

Paying close attention to nutrition facts is an important part of maintaining a healthy diet.

THE FUTURE

Grasshoppers and other insects are already a common food in some parts of the world.

THE FUTURE

What's ahead for new products that rely on food science? How about better-tasting "meat" products made from plants? Plants and animals are alike in many ways. They contain fats, protein, and certain chemicals. Food scientists are creating plant-based meat substitutes that taste more like the real thing. This could help cut down on the water and other resources needed to raise livestock.

Consumers also want new tastes, so look for more foods that combine basic flavors in new ways. Think spicy-hot combined with sweet, or more fermented ingredients in foods. More of these foods might even come in edible packaging!

THINKING OUTSIDE THE BOX

Some future foods are likely to contain insects or come from algae. Eating bugs might seem a little gross, but people all over the world have been doing it for centuries. Insects are a cheap source of protein, and they can be quite tasty. A food lab in the Netherlands has experimented with a wide range of insects to see which ones have the best flavor. In 2015, a U.S. company called Six

New milk substitutes could reduce the demand for dairy-derived milk.

Foods introduced chips made with cricket flour—dried, ground-up crickets. Another U.S. company, Solazyme, produces flour and a protein powder using algae. These ingredients can be added to other foods.

THE GROWTH OF GMOS

New breakthroughs in genetic engineering will also shape the food we eat. Though some people dislike GMOs, food scientists believe they are important for raising crops that resist disease and pests. GMOs also help address one of the world's biggest problems—figuring out how to grow enough nutritious food to feed the planet's expanding population. Some scientists are looking at ways to use genetically modified yeast to produce a drink that tastes like milk. Like meat substitutes, the new product would reduce the use of space and other resources needed to raise cows.

Food scientists and engineers address many concerns. They improve nutrition, make foods safer and tastier, and develop new technology to process foods. Since people will always need food, these innovators will always play an important part in our lives. ✳

Meat substitutes can provide important nutrients and satisfying flavors without the drawbacks of real meat.

CAREER STATS

AGRICULTURAL AND FOOD SCIENTISTS

MEDIAN ANNUAL SALARY: $58,610

NUMBER OF JOBS (2012): 38,500

PROJECTED JOB GROWTH: 9%, as fast as average

PROJECTED INCREASE IN JOBS, 2012–2022: 3,600

REQUIRED EDUCATION: At least a bachelor's degree; most scientists earn doctorate degrees

LICENSE/CERTIFICATION: Certification not usually required but desirable

AGRICULTURAL AND FOOD SCIENCE TECHNICIANS

MEDIAN ANNUAL SALARY: $34,070

NUMBER OF JOBS (2012): 25,900

PROJECTED JOB GROWTH: 3%, slower than average

PROJECTED INCREASE IN JOBS, 2012–2022: 800

REQUIRED EDUCATION: At least a high school diploma, plus on-the-job training

LICENSE/CERTIFICATION: None

CHEMISTS

MEDIAN ANNUAL SALARY: $73,060

NUMBER OF JOBS (2012): 96,200

PROJECTED JOB GROWTH: 6%, slower than average

PROJECTED INCREASE IN JOBS, 2012–2022: 5,400

REQUIRED EDUCATION: At least a bachelor's degree; most scientists earn doctorate degrees

LICENSE/CERTIFICATION: Certification not usually required

Figures reported by the United States Bureau of Labor Statistics

RESOURCES

BOOKS

Barber, Nicola. *Cloning and Genetic Engineering*. New York: Rosen Central, 2013.

Frydenborg, Kay. *Chocolate: Sweet Science and Dark Secrets of the World's Favorite Treat*. Boston: Houghton Mifflin Harcourt, 2015.

Ichord, Loretta. *Double Cheeseburgers, Quiche, and Vegetarian Burritos: American Cooking from the 1920s Through Today*. Minneapolis: Carolrhoda Books, 2014.

Katirgis, Jane. *STEM Jobs in Food and Nutrition*. Vero Beach, FL: Rourke Educational Media, 2015.

Kurlansky, Mark. *Frozen in Time: Clarence Birdseye's Outrageous Idea About Frozen Food*. New York: Delacorte Press, 2014.

Rogers, Kara. *The Science of Nutrition*. Chicago: Britannica Educational Publishing, 2013.

Taylor-Butler, Christine. *Food Safety*. New York: Children's Press, 2008.

Weiss, Ellen. *The Sense of Taste*. New York: Children's Press, 2009.

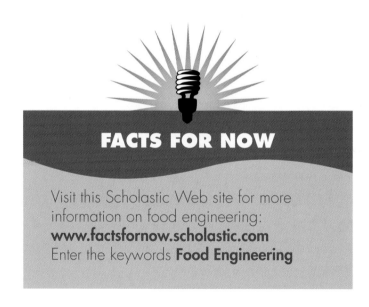

FACTS FOR NOW

Visit this Scholastic Web site for more information on food engineering:
www.factsfornow.scholastic.com
Enter the keywords **Food Engineering**

GLOSSARY

additive (AD-i-tiv) something added to a substance, especially food

bacteria (bak-TEER-ee-uh) microscopic, single-celled living things that exist everywhere and can be either useful or harmful

biochemistry (by-oh-KEM-iss-tree) the field of science that studies chemical processes that relate to living things

calories (KAL-ur-eez) a measurement of the amount of energy contained in food

carbohydrate (kahr-buh-HYE-drate) one of the substances in foods such as bread, rice, and potatoes that give you energy

contaminating (kuhn-TAM-uh-nay-ting) adding harmful or undesirable substances

dehydrated (dee-HYE-dray-tid) with the water removed

digest (dye-JEST) to break down food in the organs of digestion so that it can be absorbed into the blood and used by the body

fermentation (fur-men-TAY-shun) a chemical process that turns sugars into acids, alcohol, or gases

microorganisms (mye-kroh-OR-guh-niz-uhmz) living things that are so small they can be seen only with a microscope

nutrients (NOO-tree-uhnts) substances such as proteins, minerals, or vitamins that are needed by people, animals, and plants to stay strong and healthy

pathogens (PATH-uh-jens) microorganisms that can cause illness

pesticides (PES-ti-sidez) chemicals used to kill insects and other pests

preserve (pri-ZURV) to treat food so that it does not become spoiled

processed (PRAH-sesd) prepared or changed by a series of steps

protein (PROH-teen) a type of chemical compound found in all living plant and animal cells

prototyping (PROH-toh-type-ing) creating an early version of an invention to see if it works

species (SPEE-sheez) one of the groups into which animals and plants of the same genus are divided; members of the same species can mate and have offspring

sustainable (suh-STAY-nuh-buhl) done in a way that can be continued and that doesn't use up natural resources

INDEX

Page numbers in *italics* indicate illustrations.

INDEX

ABOUT THE AUTHOR

MICHAEL BURGAN is the author of more than 250 books for children and young adults, both fiction and nonfiction. His books on science include *Developing Flu Vaccines*, *Not a Drop to Drink: Water for a Thirsty World*, and biographies of several scientists and inventors. A graduate of the University of Connecticut with a degree in history, Burgan is also a produced playwright and the editor of *The Biographer's Craft*. He lives in Santa Fe, New Mexico. He would like to thank Matthew Cael, Rebecca Skolmutch, and Mindy Weinstein of the Institute of Food Technologists for their help with this book.